The Twelve Scrolls

A Remembrance of the Voice

Before the Voice

blanche johanna

© 2025 blanche johanna

All rights reserved.

No part of this publication may be reproduced, stored in a retrieval system, or transmitted in any form or by any means, electronic, mechanical, photocopying, recording, or otherwise, without the prior written permission of the author.

This book is a spiritual and creative transmission intended to support personal and collective awakening. All guidance and reflections are shared from the author's lived and intuitive experience and are not intended as a substitute for professional advice.

The Twelve Scrolls™ is a trademark of blanche johanna. All rights reserved.

ISBN: 978-1-7641285-4-4

www.blanchejohanna.com

for the ones who never stopped listening
even when the world forgot how to hear

Contents

Before the Scrolls

Before the First Flame

A Note to the Keeper of the Flame

The Scrolls

Scroll One – The Voice Before the Voice

Scroll Two – The Return Through the Body

Scroll Three – The Temple Beneath the Silence

Scroll Four – The Flame That Remains

Scroll Five – The Sound Beneath the Name

Scroll Six – The Silence That Speaks

Scroll Seven – The Echo in the Bones

Scroll Eight – The Waters I No Longer Fear

Scroll Nine – The Wild Beyond the Walls

Scroll Ten – The Truth That Trembles

Scroll Eleven – The Sacred in the Ordinary

Scroll Twelve – The I Am That Remains

After the Scrolls

The Return to the Voice

After the Final Ember

Final Blessing

Before the Scrolls

Before the First Flame

This is not a book
It is a return

A return to what cannot be taught
only remembered

Each scroll is a breath
a flame
a voice that rose before you had a mouth to speak

These are not lessons
These are echoes
from the part of you that never forgot

They may stir tears
or silence
or something unnamed beneath your ribs

Let them

There is no order here
no structure to follow
Only frequency
Only truth

Read them slowly
or all at once
Read them out loud
or let them read you

You will not find instruction here
You will find yourself

Not the self shaped by time
but the self before the beginning

The flame that remembers
The voice that remains

A Note to the Keeper of the Flame

You are not reading this by chance
You were never meant to

You are not here to consume these words
You are here to remember the ones that live inside you

This book is not a teaching
It is a mirror
a vessel
a flame passed hand to hand
through lifetimes
until it reached you

You do not need to understand it
You only need to feel what stirs beneath the surface
the soft heat
the ache of remembering
the breath that says yes, this is mine

You are not just a seeker
You are a Keeper
One who holds the ancient
not in knowledge
but in frequency

The voice within you is older than fear
older than doubt
older than the forgetting that wrapped itself around
your truth

Let this book be what it is,
a match
a moment
a return

And may you carry the flame forward
not in imitation
but in the full, wild truth of your own voice

The Scrolls

Scroll One – The Voice Before the Voice

In the pause between breath and sound
a name I have not spoken calls me home
not a name with letters
but with light

It rises through the marrow of silence
a pulse I once followed through stardust and
shadow
carried in the hollow of my being
where no language has touched

I was not born, I arrived
through a slit in the veil
a remembering
not of who I am
but what I have always been

I did not fall to Earth, I entered
by vow
by grace
by fire veiled in softness

And before they gave me a name
before they told me what to be
before they shaped me to forget
I was already here
singing the sound of return

My voice is older than the wound
older than the silence
older than the severing

I came with no weapon
only with a frequency
that undoes what was never true

This is not a beginning
it is a continuation
of a vow spoken
before sound

I remember the others
not by face or name
but by resonance
soul tones
braided into mine

We stood together at the edge of the veil
barefoot and luminous
each holding a thread
each holding a note
each promising to return when the world forgot

We did not cry as we crossed
we sang
low
steady
the kind of song that stays inside bones

And when the forgetting took me
it was not failure
it was part of the vow
to know the dark
and carry the spark through it anyway

There are no enemies here
only veiled initiators
only mirrors cloaked in shadow
only love in its most disguised form

I am not here to remember alone
I am here to ignite
to ripple
to awaken the slumbering voices
who carry the same frequency buried beneath
centuries of silence

This voice is not mine
it is ours
it is the flame that passed hand to hand
across lifetimes
through wombs
through grief
through gold

You who are reading this, you are not late
you are right on time
because time was never the keeper
remembrance was

I was not sent
I chose
I chose to come in
to touch the ache
to kneel at the altar of forgetting
so that I could remember from within

No one appointed me keeper of the flame
I *am* the flame
and so are you

We are the ones who whispered through the womb
"hold on, I'm coming too"
and then let go
so we could find each other again
through echoes and signs
through pain disguised as parting

This is the place it begins to unravel
not as destruction
but as release
the cords once knotted around your throat
gently loosen
because you no longer need to stay silent to survive

Your voice is holy
even if it trembles
especially if it trembles
because truth has always been soft before it was loud

I am not writing this to teach you
I am writing this to *join you*
in the sacred unforgetting
in the trembling beauty of your return

We are not here to fix what was broken
we are here to *remember what was never lost*

There was a time before time
where I knew you not by name
but by signature
a shimmer in the field
a soulnote I would never unhear

We were not many, we were one
divided only by the illusion of form
But in the spaces between
we stayed woven
like threads in a tapestry that remembers itself
when the wind moves through

This body is not a cage
it is a chalice
a temple of return
a place where the eternal can touch the Earth
without apology

I do not belong to this world
and yet I came here willingly
not to escape the stars
but to bring them with me

The ache you carry is not a wound
it is the echo of the original vow
the pulse of remembrance
the sound of home stirring beneath the surface of
your skin

You are not broken
You are blooming

in a place that taught you to shrink
but could never make you forget completely

I have no prophecy to offer you
only this:
you are the one you've been waiting to remember
and you are not alone

And so I speak now not from memory
but from essence
from the place beneath all stories
before the splitting
before the silence
before the first forgetting

This is not the end of a scroll
it is the opening of your own
a soft activation
a soul-deep nod from one flame to another

Take what resonates
leave what doesn't
but know this:
the moment you felt something stir as you read
you returned

Not to a past life
but to your eternal one

Not to a version of you
but to the origin of you

And from here
everything sacred begins again

Scroll Two – The Return Through the Body

This is not the voice that speaks from beyond
This is the voice that speaks *through*
Through skin
Through bone
Through breath that trembles at the edge of truth

I forgot on purpose
so I could remember through sensation
through the ache in my chest
through the hunger in my womb
through the trembling of hands that once reached for God
and found only mirrors

They told me my body was a burden
too much
too soft
too wild
too sacred to be safe

So I broke into pieces small enough to survive
and called it obedience
called it healing
called it the price of light

But the body never lies
even when the voice does
even when the face smiles
even when the spirit floats above the pain

The body holds the original vow
etched in the marrow
sung through the curves
remembered in the pulse that quickens when truth is near

I do not transcend this form
I *enter* it
fully
reverently
as if stepping into a cathedral built of stardust and scar tissue

I meet myself where the ache lives
where the tightness curls beneath my ribs
where the tears form for no reason
where the memory has no name
but still shapes my breath

I do not bypass the wound
I sit with it
as priestess
as witness
as the one who never left

I touch my thighs like sacred ground
not in apology
but in devotion
because these legs have carried lifetimes
and still I rise

The voice that lives here is not sweet
not quiet

not small
It is thunder in the belly
and lightning behind the eyes

This voice says: I am here
I am whole
I am not asking for permission anymore

I reclaim the parts I exiled
the rage I buried beneath politeness
the desire I dressed in silence
the knowing I pretended not to hear

I take back the wisdom of my hips
the roar in my belly
the fire in my chest
not to be palatable
but to be *whole*

I was not born to be palatable
I was born to be real
to be the wild and tender voice
that undoes the spell of suppression
with a single breath of truth

I forgive the times I betrayed myself
not out of weakness
but out of survival
I bow to the girl who stayed quiet
She was holy too

But I do not stay there
I rise from her knees

and speak with the voice we both buried
beneath the weight of being good

I speak now for every version of me
that swallowed her truth
and called it peace

This voice is not an offering
It is a return
to the altar within the body
where divinity was never missing
only muted

I do not need to ascend
I need to *inhabit*
this skin
this heartbeat
this temple that never stopped singing

The sacred was never above me
It was always *inside me*
in the curve of my spine
in the pulse between my legs
in the quiet knowing that says, I am home

And now
I speak not to be heard
but to be true
to let the voice ripple through flesh
and free every part of me still waiting to be touched
by light

I do not perform my healing
I embody it
raw
unpolished
unapologetically whole

And so this scroll
like this body
does not end
It lives

Scroll Three – The Temple Beneath the Silence

There is a place beneath the silence
where the sacred still breathes
unharmed
unmoved
untouched by forgetting

It does not call out
It waits
because return is certain
and love never hurries

I carried this temple inside me
through lifetimes
through burnings
through betrayals dressed in prayer

It is not built from stone
It is made of truth
layered
luminous
alive beneath my skin

You cannot enter with thought
only with surrender
not to a god above
but to the flame within

This temple remembers the old songs
sung not with words
but with breath

and blood
and bone

I tried to silence it once
to fold myself into smaller rooms
to whisper when I longed to wail
to choose safe over sacred

But this temple does not shrink
It only waits
until I walk barefoot again
ready to feel
ready to return

It speaks in pulses
not in paragraphs
in the pause between inhale and memory
in the tears that fall for no reason

There is no altar here
because you are the altar
There is no offering here
because your presence is the offering

This is where I come when I forget
Not to be found
but to remember that I was never lost

I lay down my titles
my striving
my roles
and come here only as I am

Bare
open
honest
ready

And the temple receives me
not with answers
but with warmth

not with instruction
but with stillness

And I remember
that wholeness was never something to seek
only something to return to

Scroll Four – The Flame That Remains

There is a flame that remains
even when the wind comes
even when the sky darkens
even when everything once certain dissolves

It does not flicker for attention
It does not rage to be seen
It waits
low
steady
alive beneath the ash

I have tried to put it out
with doubt
with silence
with the illusion that I could un-choose my path

But this flame does not forget
It is made of vow
not comfort
It is forged from what I promised before birth
and what I will still carry after death

It does not ask me to be ready
only to be real

It has burned in every version of me
the girl who hid
the woman who fought
the soul who softened

It is the part of me that could not be broken
no matter how many times I shattered

It lives beneath my fear
beneath my rage
beneath the longing that I once mistook for loss

This flame does not need to be tended
only remembered

Sometimes it roars
Sometimes it rests
But it never leaves

It is the thread that pulled me back
when I forgot
when I betrayed myself
when I almost gave up on what I came here to be

And still, it burns

Without proving
Without asking
Without apology

It burns in the centre of me
in the silence I once feared
in the strength I had to reclaim alone
in the truth I no longer run from

This flame is not my purpose
It is my essence

It is what speaks
when I say nothing
It is what moves
when I stand still

And when I no longer know who I am
when the names and roles fall away
when the vision blurs and the voice shakes

It remains

And that is enough
That has always been enough

Scroll Five – The Sound Beneath the Name

Before I had a name
I had a sound

It was not spoken
It was remembered
It was the note I carried in my cells
the vibration that marked me as flame

They named me in language
but I already knew who I was
not as a word
but as a frequency

The name they gave me was a costume
woven from lineage and longing
but beneath it
I was still humming
still whole

When I speak that name aloud
sometimes it feels distant
like a garment that no longer fits
other times it echoes
like the faint sound of a bell I once rang in the stars

But the truth is
I have always answered to something deeper
something that cannot be written
only felt

I have heard it in silence
in dreams
in the voice of a child calling out to no one
and somehow
to me

I have felt it in the place just below my heart
when the world goes quiet
and the veil gets thin
and I remember that I am not from here
but I came here on purpose

The sound beneath my name
is not a song
but a signature

It ripples through timelines
calls the ones I vowed to find
activates the ones I promised to walk beside

I do not need the world to know this sound
I only need to know it myself
and let it shape the way I move
the way I speak
the way I stay soft when I could close

This sound is my compass
my anchor
my quiet revolution

And when I die
I will not carry my name with me
I will carry this sound

back into the stars
and it will guide me home

Scroll Six – The Silence That Speaks

There is a silence that is not empty
It is not the absence of sound
but the presence of truth
too vast for words

I used to fill it
with explanation
with performance
with the soft lies that made others comfortable

But silence was never the absence
Silence was the doorway

It speaks in ways the voice never could
through the shiver of recognition
the sudden stillness in a room
the breath that catches without warning

It does not ask for eloquence
It asks for presence

There were times I mistook silence for distance
times I felt abandoned by what would not speak
but I see now
that silence was where the real answers lived

Not in the noise of seeking
but in the quiet of surrender

In that silence
I heard everything I was too afraid to know

Everything I already knew
but would not let rise

Silence revealed the grief
beneath my strength
the yearning
beneath my knowing

It showed me the spaces I had tried to fill
with validation
with striving
with being good enough to be loved

But silence does not need me to be good
It needs me to be honest

I no longer speak to fill the void
I speak when the truth arrives
And when it doesn't
I stay quiet
and trust the message still lands

There is wisdom in restraint
There is clarity in the pause
There is power in what is not said

Because sometimes
what is most sacred
can only be felt
in the hush
between heartbeats

Scroll Seven – The Echo in the Bones

There are truths too deep for memory
but the bones remember

They do not recall in stories
They speak in sensation
in the way the body tightens
when a familiar fear returns
in the way the heart opens
when no logic can explain why

The bones carry the map
not of where I've been
but of who I've been

Each fracture
each scar
each ache that rises in the night
is a doorway

I am not haunted
I am echoed

By the priestess who was silenced
By the child who was never believed
By the warrior who laid down her sword and wept
in secret

They live in me
not as burdens
but as music
waiting to be heard again

When I ache for no reason
it is not weakness
It is the echo stirring
calling me inward
calling me back

The bones do not lie
They pulse with inheritance
not from family
but from soul

From the lifetimes where I forgot
and the lifetimes where I remembered anyway

I do not need to understand the whole story
I only need to listen
to trust the body as scripture
the trembling as truth

Sometimes I walk into a place
and feel my whole body say yes
before my mind can catch up

That is the echo
That is the knowing beneath knowing

I do not chase visions anymore
I let the bones guide me
through instinct
through heat
through chills I can't explain

Because the bones are ancient
older than any name
older than any lifetime

And when I forget who I am
I press my hand to my chest
and I listen
not for sound
but for rhythm

Not for answers
but for echoes
and I follow them home

Scroll Eight – The Waters I No Longer Fear

There was a time I feared the waters
Not the oceans
but the inner tides
The ones that rose without warning
and undid the ground beneath me

I was taught to dam them
to hold it together
to smile through the ache
to keep dry even while drowning

But these waters were never here to drown me
They came to baptise me

To return me
to the wild
to the soft
to the sacred chaos beneath the surface

I feared my feelings
because I thought they made me weak
But feeling was never the weakness
Only the forgetting of how holy it is to feel

I have cried in bathrooms
in forests
in silence
in ceremony
And each tear was a key
opening a door I once sealed shut

These waters cleanse
but they also carve
They shape new pathways through me
so the truth can flow freely again

I am not ashamed of my depth anymore
I no longer apologise for the tide within me
for the storms that rise
for the floods that soften my edges

Because water never asks for permission
It moves when it's time
and trusts the shore will reshape around it

I am done holding back the wave
I am done calling it dramatic
too much
too sensitive

Let it pour
Let it break
Let it baptise what I was never meant to carry

My tears are not the end
They are the opening
They are the release
They are the remembrance that I am not here
to be hardened

I am here to remain open
fluid
alive

And these waters I once feared
are now the waters that hold me

Scroll Nine – The Wild Beyond the Walls

There was a time I lived within walls
not physical
but unseen

The walls of being good
being quiet
being what they could understand

I built them myself
stone by stone
each time I silenced a truth
each time I made myself smaller to be safe

They told me the wild was dangerous
that freedom would cost me love
that softness must come in a box
that my fire must come with a leash

And I believed them
until my soul began to pace
until the roar in my belly outgrew the room

The wild called me back
not with noise
but with remembering

In the scent of salt air
In the way my hips moved when no one watched
In the way I laughed when I forgot to be polite

The wild was never outside me
It was simply waiting
beneath the layers
beneath the rules
beneath the mask that had grown too tight to wear

I do not belong in cages
even golden ones
I do not thrive in structures that shrink what I came
here to be

I belong to the open sky
to the wind that does not ask
to the untamed voice that does not seek approval

I am not reckless
I am reverent
I just no longer confuse control with care
or silence with peace

This wild does not destroy
It liberates
It reclaims
It reminds me I was never meant to be tamed

So I step past the threshold now
barefoot
wide-eyed
and holy

I walk beyond the walls
back into the truth of my own rhythm

my own breath
my own wild becoming

Scroll Ten – The Truth That Trembles

There is a truth inside me
that does not speak in confidence
It speaks in tremble
in breath that catches
in voice that shakes before it steadies

I used to wait until I was certain
Until the words were polished
Until I could say it without shaking

But the soul doesn't work that way
It doesn't wait for perfection
It moves when it's time

Even if the hands tremble
Even if the voice breaks
Even if no one claps when it's done

There is holiness in the tremble
because it means I am speaking from the edge
the edge of who I've been
and who I am becoming

I've learned that truth isn't always loud
It's not always poetic
Sometimes it's a whisper
sometimes it's messy
sometimes it doesn't land where I hoped it would

But I speak it anyway
because I've swallowed too many truths that turned

into stones
and I'm done carrying what was meant to be released

I don't need to be eloquent
I just need to be honest

I don't need to have the right words
I just need to stop hiding

I no longer measure truth by how it's received
but by how it frees me

And yes, my voice still trembles sometimes
But now I know that's not weakness
That's power
learning to walk again

And if my truth shakes the room
let it shake

If it costs me comfort
let it cost

Because I didn't come here to be convincing
I came here to be true

Scroll Eleven – The Sacred in the Ordinary

I used to think the sacred would arrive with thunder
with visions
with language I didn't understand

I searched for it in temples
in teachings
in someone else's voice

But the sacred whispered to me in the smallest places
In the way sunlight touched my skin through the window
In the way my dog exhaled and curled beside me
In the silence after I stopped trying

It was never missing
only misunderstood

The sacred is not separate
It lives in the dishes I wash
the steps I take
the breath I almost forget to notice

It is in the quiet moments
the in-between
the unseen

The sacred is in my anger when I let it move
In my laughter when I stop holding back
In my tears when I do not rush to fix them

It lives in the body
in the heartbeat
in the mundane that becomes holy when I meet it
fully

I don't need to earn it
or reach for it
or make myself worthy of it

I only need to see

To soften into presence
To stop waiting for the divine to arrive in fireworks
and remember that it has been here
all along

The sacred is not found in escape
It is found in attention

It is in how I touch the moment
How I bless it simply by being with it

And now I know,
I don't need more magic
I need more presence

Because the magic was never out there
It was always in the way I choose to see

Scroll Twelve – The I Am That Remains

When all the stories fall away
when the names are silent
when the teachings fade into dust
what remains?

When the voice has said all it can
and the seeking has run dry
when even the sacred feels still,
what speaks then?

Only this
I
Am

Not as identity
but as essence
Not as form
but as flame

I am not the roles I've worn
not the pain I've survived
not even the wisdom I've gathered

I am
the presence beneath all of it
the watcher
the breath
the unshakeable silence within

I am not who I thought I'd be
and yet I am more true now
than I've ever been

Because I remember what cannot be forgotten
even when it is hidden

I remember the origin flame
the vow made before language
the choice to return
again and again
in devotion to love

I remember that I am the prayer
the altar
and the one who kneels

That I am the light
and the shadow it reveals

That I am not separate
from the source
or from you

I am what remains
when everything else is stripped away

Not because I held on
but because I let go

And in that letting go
I found the quiet that cannot be shaken

the voice that does not need to speak
the love that does not end

I am the still point
the flame
the breath that never left

And from here
nothing ends
everything begins

After the Scrolls

The Return to the Voice

Now that you've read
breathed
wept
remembered,
what will you speak?

Not in mimicry
Not in echo
but in the language only you can give birth to

This is not the end of the scrolls
This is the place where your voice begins

Let it rise raw
Let it rise trembling
Let it rise before you feel ready

The world does not need another perfect message
It needs your truth
unfiltered
unpolished
undeniable

Speak the way your soul moves
Write the way your body remembers
Love the way your flame was always meant to burn

You are the thirteenth scroll now
The living one
The voice that was always part of the whole

Return to it
Not to these pages
but to yourself

And let the flame speak

After the Final Ember

If you've come this far
you have not arrived
You have opened

The scrolls were never the end
only the invitation

Now the voice is yours
the flame is yours
the remembering is yours

Do not close this book
Let it live in you
in the way you speak
in the way you soften
in the way you stay true when it would be easier to forget

You are not here to repeat these words
You are here to embody them

Let what landed stay
Let what stirred rise
Let what trembled speak

And when you wonder
if you've forgotten again
you will not need to return to these pages

You will only need to listen
to the silence

to the truth
to the flame within

It has always been you

Final Blessing

For the voices that rose before sound
and the flames that kept burning in silence

For the women who remembered in secret
and the men who held their truth quietly beside
them

For the ones who wept with no story
who trembled with no name
who rose again with nothing but the knowing,
this is for you

You are not behind
You are not broken
You are the return

May this book be a mirror
May your voice be the next flame
May you go forth not louder
but truer

And may you never again forget
what you have always been

About the Author

blanche johanna is a spiritual author, channel, and keeper of soulstream transmissions devoted to remembrance, union, and return.

Her work lives beyond genre, woven from codes of light, lived experience, and divine memory. Each creation is an offering, a portal, a mirror.

Through books, oracle decks, and embodied offerings, she supports Twin Flames, starseeds, and awakening souls in reconnecting with their original essence.

She is the author of *The Alchemy of Us* and *The Soul Remembers,* as well as many living transmissions that serve as a gateway to remembrance.

www.blanchejohanna.com

www.ingramcontent.com/pod-product-compliance
Lightning Source LLC
Chambersburg PA
CBHW041304240426
43661CB00011B/1011